"Asia Has Claims
Upon New England"

"Asia Has Claims Upon New England"

Assyrian Reliefs at Yale

Sam Harrelson

Yale University Art Gallery, New Haven, Connecticut

Sam Harrelson

Asia Has Claims Upon New England: Assyrian Reliefs at Yale

Copyright © 2006 Yale University Art Gallery
P.O. Box 208271
New Haven, CT 06520-8271

This publication is made possible by The Andrew W. Mellon
Foundation and the Mary Cushing Fosburgh and James
Whitney Fosburgh, B.A. 1933, M.A. 1935, Publication Fund

ISBN #0-89467-965-1

Harrelson, Sam B.

Asia has claims upon New England : Assyrian reliefs at Yale / Sam
B. Harrelson.

p.cm.

Includes bibliographical references.

ISBN #0-89467-965-1

1. Relief (Sculpture), Assyro-Babylonian—Catalogs. 2. Relief
(Sculpture)—Connecticut—New Haven—Catalogs. 3. Yale University.
Art Gallery—Catalogs. 4. Relief (Sculpture), Assyro-Babylonian
—Collectors and collecting—United States—History—19th century.
I. Yale University. Art Gallery. II. Title.

NB80.H37 2006

732'.5—dc22 2006012588

Cover: Relief of an Eagle-Headed *Apkallu,* Assyrian, Palace
of Assurnasirpal II, 9th century B.C.
Alabaster. Yale University Art Gallery. 1854.3 (detail) (photograph: Alex
Contreras)

FOREWORD

THE ALABASTER RELIEFS FROM the palace of the Assyrian king Assurnasirpal II that the Yale University Art Gallery acquired in 1854 are among the University's greatest treasures. The story of their acquisition, blending a fabled ancient culture, hot desert sands, and a devoted American missionary, reflects the important role that religious thought played in bringing ancient Near Eastern art to America. Sam Harrelson (M.A.R. 2002) is uniquely qualified to present the Gallery's Assyrian bas-reliefs in the context of the missionary climate of mid-nineteenth-century America, as well as within the framework of palace art of ancient Assyria. I am grateful to Sam for bringing his special perspective to this project and believe that it will enrich the reader's experience of these extraordinary works of ancient art.

I am also grateful to Benjamin K. Foster, Laffan Professor of Assyriology at Yale, and Samuel M. Paley, Professor of Classics at the University at Buffalo, State University of New York, for reading the manuscript and offering sage and helpful advice to its author. Professor Paley's visit to the Gallery to examine the reliefs with us revealed much. Elizabeth Hendrick's analysis of the surviving traces of ancient pigment, as part of a comprehensive study of such pigments that she and Professor Paley have undertaken, restored for us much more of the vibrant original appearance of these sculptures than could ever be seen by the naked eye. Professor Paley's evocative reconstructions of palace interiors, one of which he and his associate Donald H. Sanders, President of Learning Sites, Inc., have kindly given permission to include here, put the viewer in the room with these kings, courtiers, and genies with vivid clarity. I am truly grateful to these generous scholars for their interest and kind assistance with this project. My warmest thanks are also offered to Joyce Ippolito for her impeccable editing of the manuscript, to Sonia Shannon for her beautiful design of the book, to Thames Printing Co. and especially to Judy Zimmer for their flawless execution of the publication, and to Megan Doyon, Senior Museum Assistant in Ancient Art at the Gallery, for her patience and encouragement in seeing the book through.

Susan B. Matheson
Chief Curator
The Molly and Walter Bareiss Curator of Ancient Art

PREFACE

THE YALE UNIVERSITY ART GALLERY'S collection includes a series of bas-reliefs from the palace of Assurnasirpal II, ruler of Assyria from 883 to 859 B.C. The reliefs entered the collection in 1854 and were the first acquisitions of ancient art made by the University. The following serves as a brief introduction to these bas-reliefs, both in ninth-century B.C. Assyria and in the United States in the nineteenth century A.D.

Numerous institutions in the United States now possess bas-reliefs that once decorated the walls of Assyrian palaces in ancient Mesopotamia. Many of these reliefs were acquired from Assurnasirpal II's palace at Nimrud during British excavations from 1845 to 1855. A large number of the bas-reliefs left their ancient sites and now reside in exhibition spaces in various mid-Atlantic and New England colleges with religious ties, among them Yale, Bowdoin, Williams, Amherst, Dartmouth, Middlebury, the Union Seminary in Utica, New York, and the Virginia Theological Seminary. For a short period, competition for these bas-reliefs was fierce in the desiccated countryside outside of the city of Mosul in present-day northern Iraq. Missionaries, acting as procurers of bas-reliefs and various curiosities, sought to ship to their alma maters and patrons as many objects as their respective colleges could afford or wanted. Most of these objects were shipped to the United States in the early 1850s. What drove these institutions into competition for Assyrian bas-reliefs at this time, and why was it so important to relocate these antiquities to places of higher education in the United States? These questions are essential for understanding the significance of these sculptures to institutions like Yale. At the same time, these bas-reliefs also represent an opportunity to understand U.S. religious and cultural history.

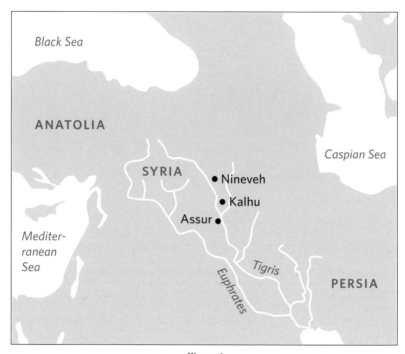

Figure 1

Assurnasirpal II

THE STATE OF ASSYRIA OCCUPIED what is now northern Iraq, in the up-per Mesopotamian region, but it varied in size. At its largest, Assyria reached from the Zagros mountain range in the east and southern Babylonia to the Mediterranean and Egypt. The inhabitants of the region were dependent on the Tigris for agricultural production (Fig. 1). The river was prone to periodic flooding, which fertilized the flood plain of the Tigris. In times of drought, however, the production of food could be seriously diminished. Elaborate systems of canals were constructed in the vicinities of the capital cities of As-sur, Nineveh, and Nimrud to bring in water for orchards and gardens from the surrounding mountains. Fertility of the land was a critical issue in food production and subsistence and thus was important in religious and civic life and symbolism.

The surrounding region was not politically stable. Warfare with border-ing states was common. Assyrian kings led annual campaigns to acquire more land and stabilize the areas already controlled. The Assyrian empire expanded and contracted with each military success and failure.

In the ninth century B.C. Assurnasirpal II constructed a new capital at Nimrud (ancient Kalhu) with a splendid palace incorporating a program of decorative bas-reliefs that assured visiting foreign dignitaries and his own people of his power and might.

Figure 2

The palace of Ashur-nasir-pal, chief-priest of Ashur, the chosen
one of Enlil and Ninurta, the favorite of Anu and Dagan, the divine
weapon of the Great Gods, the potent king, the king of the world,
the king of Assyria . . . who has no rival among the princes of the
four quarters of the earth; [who is] the shepherd of his people, fear-
less in battle . . . subjugator of the unsubmissive, who rules the total
sum of all humanity . . . I built thereon [a palace with] halls of cedar, cypress, juniper, boxwood, teak, terebinth, and tamarisk [?] as
my royal dwelling and for the enduring leisure life of my lordship.
Beasts of the mountains and the seas, which I had fashioned out of
white limestone and alabaster, I had set up in its gates. I made it [the
palace] fittingly imposing. I bordered them all around with bronze
studs. I mounted doors of cedar, cypress, juniper, and terebinth in
its gates.

So read sections of the cuneiform text known as the Standard Inscription,
which was carved across each individual slab in Assurnasirpal II's Northwest
Palace at Kalhu (Calah in the Old Testament book of *Genesis*). The inscrip-

tion, in its entirety, tells the story of the king's lineage, his potency as king and protector of Assyria, his status as high priest to the gods, his ferocity in battle, and the building of his palace at Kalhu. This palace, from which the bas-reliefs in the Yale collection come, was an undertaking of enormous proportions and required resources and funding of an impressive magnitude. Renowned for its military might, as related in such biblical books as *Chronicles*, *Kings*, and *Isaiah*, Assyria carried out an aggressive campaign of conquering lands and people to acquire its vast resources. Building this new capital at Kalhu was a symbol of power and might not only of the Assyrian state but also of King Assurnasirpal II.

Assurnasirpal II (Fig. 2) came to the Assyrian throne upon the death of his father, Tukulti-Ninurta II, in 884 B.C. Assyria's military and economic power had sharply declined from its pinnacle in the early twelfth century B.C., and it was embroiled in regional disputes with a strengthening Babylonia and various neighboring tribes. Before his death, Tukulti-Ninurta II was able to stabilize a southern border with Babylonia and prepare for a campaign into the commercially and agriculturally rich area of northwest Mesopotamia. By the ninth century B.C., Assyria already had a rich legacy of conquests and powerful kings, stretching back to the twelfth century B.C. The memory of a powerful past never left the minds of later Assyrian kings. whose palace construction was closely related to that of twelfth-century palaces. By the reign of Tukulti-Ninurta II, the Assyrians were eager to return their empire to its former glory.

After becoming king, Assurnasirpal began a series of annual conquests to shore up his power over areas already controlled by Assyria. Assurnasirpal was ferocious in battle and was driven by the desire to expand the empire westward. His spectacular new palace reasserted the glory of Assyria. In the fifth year of his reign, he began a series of operations to conquer the land west of the Euphrates River. Doing so would provide him with the material resources and manpower to build temples and palaces at Nineveh, Assur, and Kalhu.

At about the same time, Assurnasirpal moved the capital of Assyria from the city of Assur to Kalhu. Kalhu's surrounding wall was 7.5 km in circumference and included nine temples in addition to the new palace. The palace itself was quite large, reaching approximately 550 feet from north to south and 200 feet from east to west (Fig. 3). Large courtyards and apartments, including two throne rooms (Fig. 5), composed the Northwest Palace, so named in

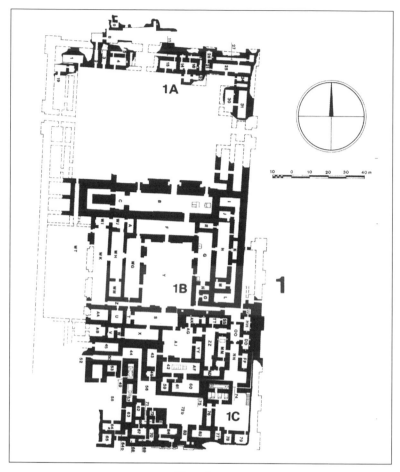

Figure 3

modern times because of its position relative to the citadel of the city. Workers were imported from the surrounding countryside and other cities to construct the new capital and palace (and eventually came to reside there).

The large colossal bull or lion figures with human heads that are so identifiable with Assyrian palaces to the modern viewer marked the various entrances to the palace apartments (Fig. 5). These figures are astounding in their detail, but the most fascinating feature is the fifth leg, which adds the notion of

Figure 4

movement to the guardians of the palace. A visitor to the palace would get the sense that the colossi were striding, ready to protect the king and the state of Assyria. Similar colossi would be replicated in palaces of Assurnasirpal's descendants, who understood the power and might the figures expressed. Later Assyrian palaces also repeated the programs of brightly painted stone reliefs that lined the walls of Assurnasirpal's palace. These bas-reliefs were found on the walls of the principal suites of the Northwest Palace (Fig. 3). Carved across them, in the Akkadian cuneiform script, was the Standard Inscription mentioned earlier.

The bas-reliefs in the Northwest Palace were not only decorative. They were visual representations of ideas about King Assurnasirpal and Assyria (Fig. 5, pp. 8–9). The bas-reliefs are arranged in rows, or registers, and often

Figure 5

Figure 6

represent a significant theme from among the king's activities. These themes
vary from room to room, perhaps to represent different functions for each
room. For instance, some bas-reliefs show Assurnasirpal doing such things as
hunting (and killing) lions with bow and arrow or spear. In the same rooms
with the hunting scenes, assumed to be the throne rooms of the palace, military campaigns also make up part of the bas-relief program. Scholars inter-
pret these scenes as showing Assurnasirpal's power over both the animal and
human threats to Assyria. In other rooms, commonly thought to have been
shrines to the gods, bas-reliefs depict processionals and offerings of libations
(as in rooms F, G, H in Fig. 3).

Another program of bas-reliefs, including the group from which three
of the examples in the Yale collection derive, shows various figures performing some act of ritual on a stylized palm tree (Fig. 13). Figures depicted vary
in size and form from the bearded and unbearded to the bird-headed and
winged. Their common trait is the act they are performing on the stylized tree.
In most of these bas-reliefs, as in the ones at Yale, figures hold a pail or a bucket
in one hand and a cone-shaped object in the other. The figures' depiction may
seem awkward, but it is, in fact, a masterful articulation of human movement.
Scholars have suggested that the figures are purifying or fertilizing the stylized
date tree using the cone after it has been dipped in the pail, probably contain-
ing some sort of holy water or pollen (Fig. 7). The various *apkallu*-figures,
or guardian spirits, often called genii, were common to Near Eastern art and
religion. There are numerous portrayals of them on cylinder seals and other
small artifacts from before, during, and after the period of Assurnasirpal II's
reign. Genii were seen as divine spirits who protected the land and people

and guarded against evil spirits. The genii's performance of this ritual on the stylized tree symbolically protected and strengthened Assyria and the king. In some relief panels, the stylized tree is replaced by the figure of Assurnasirpal II while the guardian spirits continue to perform the ritual act with the cone and pail. The depiction of the stylized or Sacred Tree probably represents Assyria, so the country and the king are therefore protected and nourished by the guardian spirits, just as the colossal human-headed bulls and lions protect the palace itself. The substitution of the king for the Sacred Tree is strong evidence for this interpretation.

In general, the programs of bas-relief show Assurnasirpal as a priestly worshipper and overseer of agriculture, fertility, and the state of Assyria. He is portrayed as warrior, hunter, administrator, and chief intercessor between humans and the gods. The multivalent natures of Assurnasirpal's reign and his goals as monarch are presented in the various themes shown on the stone slabs.

The guardian spirits and giant human-headed bulls and lions protected Assurnasirpal II and his Northwest Palace at Kalhu well. Assurnasirpal ruled long and successfully and he expanded the borders of the empire. Kalhu remained the capital of Assyria until Sargon II (721–705 B.C.) built his capital at Dur Sharrukin (modern Khorsabad).

Figure 7

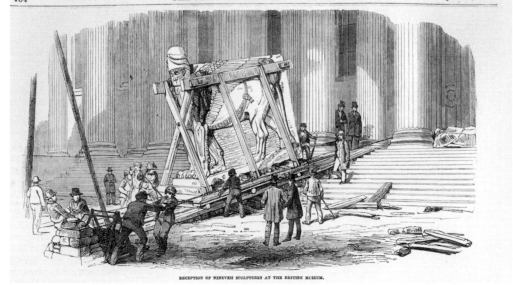

RECEPTION OF NINEVEH SCULPTURES AT THE BRITISH MUSEUM.

Figure 8

Discovery

IN 1845, A TWENTY-EIGHT-YEAR-OLD British diplomat and adventurer, Austen Henry Layard, sailed down the Tigris River en route to Baghdad. Along the way, he was sidetracked by the alluring, raised tells along the riverbank, which stood apart from the otherwise flat landscape. He soon returned to lead an archaeological expedition. Trouble with local authorities concerning digging and fights over acquisitions, however, forced the work to be done mostly at night by torches. Soon, his tunnel digging put him squarely in the dark faces of genii and eagle-headed figures from the ninth century B.C.; he had found the Northwest Palace of Assurnasirpal II. Amazed at his discovery, he quickly gained permission to keep digging. He led a vigorous publicity crusade, which sparked a bout of "Assyromania" in Britain and resulted in numerous highly successful publications, including his Monuments of Nineveh in 1849. Images such as Layard's reconstruction of Assurnasirpal's throne room (Fig. 9, pp. 14–15) captured the Victorian public's imagination, reinforced by newspaper reports and the incredibly popular debut of five sculptures in the British Museum in 1848, with a reported 900,000 visitors. Other sculptures followed as Layard continued his work (Fig. 8).

Additional monies poured into Near Eastern archaeology, and within a few years of Layard's discoveries, the Black Obelisk of the Assyrian king Shalmaneser III (with a depiction of the emissary of the Israelite king Jehu) was

Figure 9

discovered, the Assyrian language deciphered, and Sennacherib's account of the attacks against the biblical towns of Lachish and Jerusalem (as told in the biblical book of *Kings*) translated.

William F. Williams
and the Nineteenth Century

NEWS OF THE DISCOVERY OF THE PALACE and its bas-relief decoration reached America rapidly. Victorians had been quick to appreciate the unique nature of these artifacts, seeing them as provocative, even erotic, appropriations of "Oriental" cultures. It was the American Reverend Dwight Marsh, however, who first realized the religious potential that the bas-reliefs being excavated by Layard at Nimrud possessed. American missionaries were more interested in the examples that depicted rituals and divinities than in the bull colossi and other relics the British Museum had taken away. Both types of artifacts displayed the magnitude of Assyrian power, but the figures on the bas-reliefs represented their "heathen" religion and the gods that fell to the power of God.

In a letter dated November 29, 1882, some thirty years after the excavations, Marsh wrote:

> I was the only American in Mosul from the Spring of 1850 to that
> of 1851. It was the last year of Layard's stay there, and he was very
> polite and kind to me as the only representative of my country oc-
> casionally inviting me to dine with him, once about sundown on the

William Frederic Williams

Figure 10

roof of his house in Mosul: at other times asking me to breakfast and to visit him in his quarters at Nineveh or Nimrood: and whenever new treasures of sculpture were found asking me to enjoy the new sights in the trenches.

Finding him to be a great admirer and friend of America, it occurred to me in mentioning how many in our land were reading his works to suggest that my Alma Mater would be very glad to get some samples of the sculptures at Nimrood where I knew that there were duplicates. He at once offered to put two as good slabs as the best at my disposal the only drawback being their close likeness to a pair already in the British Museum.

Layard, always eager to promote the finds he was making, quickly agreed to help send some bas-reliefs to Marsh's alma mater, Williams College. But Marsh was interested in more than just their appeal to the American public. He, along with a growing number of missionaries and church leaders, saw their potential as tools to convince young Americans to join the ministry. After all, what better recruitment poster for the mission field was there than proof of the Almighty's destruction of a powerful and feared ancient empire like Assyria? In a letter from Mosul in August 1855 Marsh wrote to Reverend Mark Hopkins (president of Williams College):

My great desire is that students who look upon the relics of the past may think wisely of time and be led to take a deeper interest in the efforts made to rescue the degraded from the beastliness of their present life, and the eternal dangers impending. Would that every active imagination would hear the stones cry out, "Asia has claims upon New England!" When the young American beholds in your cabinet "the glory of the incorruptible God changed into an image made like to corruptible man, and to birds, and four footed beasts and creeping things," may their hearts be stirred within them as Paul's was at Athens. May they remember that God is older than the ages—that the glorious future of America is not eternity.

Marsh also sent "duplicates" of the bas-reliefs presented to Williams College to the Mercantile Library of St. Louis and to the Connecticut Historical Society at Hartford "with the hope of exciting a wider missionary interest."

Competition for similar examples from the palace became intense as more American missionaries sought to procure them for sponsoring colleges or their alma maters. In his August 1855 letter, Dwight Marsh also wrote, "During my absence in America slabs were quite unexpectedly obtained for Yale and Amherst. Although I arrived here before they started I could not consistently claim a share." The slabs destined for Yale are the very bas-reliefs that are now on display in the Gallery.

Through a series of letters exchanged in 1852 and 1853, Reverend William Frederic Williams (Fig. 10), in Mosul, and Reverend Leonard Bacon, in New Haven, arranged for the purchase and transport to Connecticut of examples of the wall relief and various objects from the ruins at Nimrud. Williams had been a sporadic member of the Yale faculty but decided to join the mission field in the Near East.

Williams and Bacon were already close friends, and Bacon spent some time with the missionaries as a part of the American Board of Commissioners for Foreign Missions in the Near East (ABCFM). During Bacon's trip, Williams was sent by the Western Turkey Mission to Mosul (now in northern Iraq) in order to provide aid to the established missionary there, Reverend Dwight Marsh. He had learned of the ABCFM decision to send him to Mosul in the fall of 1850. The move, which necessitated a long trip, had not been anticipated, and Reverend Williams lingered in Beirut with his wife for twenty months before finally leaving in the spring, after the birth of their daughter Cornelia.

Williams and his traveling party arrived in Mosul on a Friday evening, May 16, 1851. The sun was going down and the temperature remained at well above what was comfortable. The journey from Beirut across the Syrian Desert had taken seven weeks, and they had crossed over 450 miles in circumstances that were taxing for the group, which included his ailing wife, a small toddler, and the newborn baby. Williams rode on horseback while his wife and baby were carried on a bier drawn by mules. Bacon and his family, in the area on a relatively short trip, accompanied the Williamses' traveling company, along with numerous hired hands who handled luggage, mules, and provisions for the long and difficult trek across the desert.

Reverend Williams integrated himself into Mosul quickly and began tutoring sessions to develop his Arabic language skills. The one-tenth of Mosul residents who were Christian spoke Arabic, so Williams felt it was essential and inevitable that he pick up the language. Soon after Williams had established himself in the town, the man he was sent to relieve left on a three-month trip to Persia, taking with him Bacon and his family. Having come to the assistance of a sole missionary in a border town (distant even for the ABCFM's reach), Williams now found himself in the position of being the sole missionary. Around this time, Williams penned these words:

> As the matter is already settled, I cheerfully acquiesce in their [the board's] decision. Had the decision been made a year earlier, I should not have come to Mosul; as it is, I am content that a Providence wiser than human wisdom has ordered my lot amid these heats. I think we shall conclude to live while we can last at Mosul summer and winter, and when we melt let others come and fill our places. I hope a suitable physician may soon be found for us. I have just had the responsibility of carrying my family through ophthalmia. Mrs. Williams does not recover from the journey but is subject to severe attacks as upon the road, and staying in a convent eight hours from Mosul, a favorite pleasure resort. It was well we came for until the house I have hired is put in repair we have no safe or eligible place in the city.

Williams's problems and tribulations in Mosul continued, and he learned from letters that his brother and father had passed away. The news was difficult to bear, but content with his circumstances, he realized that an extended period of grieving would do little. The hard work of being a missionary on the frontier had to go on, along with his Arabic lessons. He continued the work with his fledgling congregation, and he had around twenty persons attending services (held twice on Sunday, as well as on Wednesday and Saturday evenings). Due to the poor weather in Mosul, however, Mrs. Williams soon developed influenza and Reverend Williams himself had to undergo surgery for piles.

After his recovery, Williams accompanied a fellow missionary, Reverend Henry Lobdell (an Amherst undergraduate and Yale Medical School graduate), to the mounds of ancient cities that surrounded Mosul. Soon, Lobdell began to offer bas-relief slabs to his alma mater, Amherst. Williams himself began to find interest among other American colleges for similar examples through correspondence. In a letter to Dr. Bacon in New Haven, dated June 15, 1853, housed in the Yale University Art Gallery archives, Williams writes about acquiring and sending some slabs to the United States:

> I acted upon the supposition that there were enough for all [Yale, Union Seminary in Utica, and Amherst]. Mr. Rassam assured me over and over that there were at least 60 slabs left and though I did not believe that—yet judging from what I had seen and from the repeated assurance that there were one or two trenches which I had not seen uncovered, I did believe that there were enough to spare. The French were in ahead of us and got five slabs and we found only three varieties left. Dr. Lobdell on behalf of Amherst insisted upon having an equal chance with Yale and Union. We of course could not go to the Mound as rival claimants and so as one party we brought away six slabs and divided them into three lots as evenly as we could and then I chose first for Yale, second for union and third went to Amherst.

In the same letter, Williams notifies Bacon that he had secured for Yale a eunuch, half of a Sacred Tree, a horned-headed divinity, a small nisroch (Fig. 11, detail), a small kneeling figure, and a brick from "the pyramid at Nimrod" along with a few cylinder seals and personal effects for friends back in New Haven.

Figure 11

Williams decided to saw the slabs, which were about a foot thick, down by two-thirds and cut them into thirds to make them easier for transportation on the backs of camels. The reliefs were packed in wooden crates with cotton at three cents a pound, which Williams (always frugal) figured "would sell for about the same in New Haven." Their transportation was another question entirely, requiring the decision of whether to send them over water, down the Tigris to the Persian Gulf and then around Africa by the Cape and then across the Atlantic to New York City, or over land, to the Mediterranean and then to America. The eventual decision was to send them across the desert by camel to the Mediterranean coast, and then across the Atlantic to New York aboard a ship named the *Wolf*.

In the letter, Williams is intent on letting Yale know that the reason he agreed to secure these objects for the University revolves around his personal relationship with Bacon. He writes:

> Yale is under obligation to you for her share of the slabs, for my let-
> ter in the first place and all my subsequent labor in the service has

been done simply from personal feelings towards yourself. It has been most gladly, most cheerfully done and it has been a source of pleasure that I could do anything for you in return for all that I have owed to you and therefore I want Yale to know that their indebtedness is to Dr. Bacon only for the opportunity of getting Nimrod slabs to New Haven. The boxes I address to your name.

If only I were able, it would give me more pleasure than you can guess if I could make a bucksheesh of the whole expense, but it is only the rich who are privileged with such luxuries. The newly located Crystal Palace in England has sent out a large order for slabs and therefore I doubt if it will be possible for any American to get any more—indeed we were told there were left nothing but the one sort, the horned headed deity which now has its representative at Williams, Yale, Amherst and Union, if these boxes only reach their destination safely. If we could have found another fillit or eunuch or nisroch we would have taken it, but we could not—though I have a sort of suspicion that there are those who know where more can be found, but I may be mistaken.

Concerned about the fate of the stones once they reached America, Williams goes on to say:

Don't let those who wash, in their zeal, wash off the black paint of hair and beard nor the black and red of the shoes as that is as old as Sardanapalus nor dig out the white of the eye for the same reason.

Unfortunately, despite his warning, the only traces of paint visible to the naked eye that survive on the Yale bas-reliefs are traces of red and black on the sandals of two of the figures (Fig. 12, pp. 24–25).

Reverend Williams dealt with Colonel Henry Rawlinson in the acquisition of these examples for Yale. Rawlinson would gain fame as one of the first translators of a complete inscription in the Assyrian language, which led directly to the study of Assyriology beginning in the mid-nineteenth century.

The bas-reliefs, shipped on the *Wolf*, arrived safely in New York Harbor on a cold winter night. Yale had paid $212 for their purchase, shipment, and

23

bribes, out of the $250 sent to Williams. Soon after their shipment, more excavations at Nimrud uncovered several more carved slabs. Williams offered some of these to Yale if more money could be allocated, but Yale decided it had spent enough on Assyrian bas-reliefs.

Bacon's interest in getting the bas-reliefs to Yale was part of a larger concern in nineteenth-century America: the hope that the figures from these ancient palaces would inspire confidence in the record of interpreted biblical history and prophecy. Many of the missionaries who saw these and other Assyrian objects immediately considered them to be proof of the accounts of books of the Bible, such as *Isaiah*.

In addition to missionary training, American universities and divinity schools, including Yale, had already established programs in biblical scholarship by the early nineteenth century. In Europe, it was a time of great unrest and tension in the realm of religion and religious studies. In the aftermath of the Enlightenment, rationalistic thinkers tested long-standing values and theories against new scientific theory. German universities, like Tübingen, gave rise to critical biblical scholarship by adopting numerous approaches to the Bible, including history, literary theory, anthropology, and the emerging field of archaeology. As this increasingly scientific and secular approach to biblical

Figure 12

literature and history influenced more American scholars and seminarians, the ideas and presuppositions of the past came into conflict with the new discoveries, creating a period of heated debate concerning the very essence of faith, belief, and authority of Scripture. This dispute found its greatest source of fuel in the question of the Bible's quality of being literally true. Those who held that the Bible was the complete word of God and inherently infallible found great fault with scholars and ministers willing to adapt the tools of scientific inquiry (in such fields as history or anthropology) to the study of the Bible.

With the increase of knowledge concerning the Near East in the nineteenth century, the debate grew even more passionate. With each new discovery of a city, artifact, or tablet with inscriptions, such as the Enuma Elish (the Babylonian Epic of Creation), or the Epic of Gilgamesh (in which the Babylonian account of the flood story in Genesis is found), it seemed that the whole basis for scriptural historical authenticity was deteriorating. Believers in the infallibility of the Bible searched for some evidence supporting the historicity of biblical accounts of history. With the discoveries of Sir Austen Henry Layard at Nineveh and Nimrud in the palaces of the Assyrian kings, one of which was the Northwest Palace of Assurnasirpal II, they felt that this evidence had been found.

Church leaders and college presidents valued these bas-reliefs both as incentives for young men to join the missionary fields and as literal proof of the word of God, as found in *Isaiah's* prophecies concerning the destruction of the Assyrians:

> Thus says the LORD: Do not be afraid because of the words that you have heard, with which the servants of the king of Assyria have reviled me. Behold, I will put a spirit in him, so that he shall hear a rumor, and return to his own land; and I will make him fall by the sword in his own land. (*Isaiah* 37.6–7)

> And the Assyrian shall fall by the sword, not of man; and a sword, not of man shall devour him; and he shall flee from the sword, and his young men shall be put to forced labor. His rock shall pass away in terror . . . (*Isaiah* 31.8–9)

There was thus another appeal of these bas-reliefs and relics besides their value in convincing young Americans to become missionaries. College presidents and church leaders saw them as tangible proof that the word of God had historical merit. In 1857, Edward Hitchcock, president of Amherst College, said, "Every new discovery of these lost cities is a new testimony to the truth of Scripture. Blessed be God that he opened this new source of Biblical history just at the period when infidelity supposed that history was proved to be false."

Yale's acquisition of Assyrian bas-reliefs from Assurnasirpal's Northwest Palace is directly attributable to the debate between religion and science in the mid-1800s. Although the reliefs inspire relatively few, if any, to become missionaries today, and the immediate connection between these sculptures and the Bible is not as pressing as it was 150 years ago, these bas-reliefs still have claims upon New England.

The Yale Reliefs

RELIEF OF AN *APKALLU*

Preserved in this bas-relief is a winged, human-headed protective spirit, or *apkallu*, wearing a three-horned helmet or mitre, a short tunic, and a heavy fringed and embroidered cloak, armed with daggers, and carrying a cone and a bucket (Fig. 14). The figure would have served a ritual duty, purifying or fertilizing a stylized and possibly Sacred Tree, which stands to the left. His action would have been a part of a larger ritual context. There have been various suggestions about where the relief was originally placed in the Northwest Palace, but many scholars place it in Room S (see Figs. 3, 13). The bas-relief is typical of the subjects in Room S and T—namely, the human-headed figure wearing the three-horned helmet. Small, floral ornamentation incised into the garment also helps to place this relief in Room S because of the absence of such decoration in Room T. Similar small incisions can be seen on the garments of several figures in Room S. When excavating these bas-reliefs, Layard made careful drawings of such incisions.

Half of the right side of a Sacred Tree remains to the left of the figure, while only the palmettes of another remain to the figure's right. At seven feet, six and a half inches tall by six feet wide, this relief is certainly impressive in

Figure 13

Reliefs from Room S

Reliefs from Room S

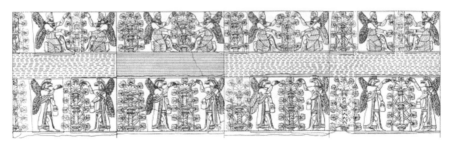

Reliefs from Room I

Figure 14

size (as well as technique) and conveys the power over the viewer that Assurnasirpal was hoping to achieve. Black and red paint is still visible to the eye
on the sandals (Fig. 12), serving as a reminder that these bas-reliefs were once
bright with painted colors.

The *apkallu* wears the ceremonial garments common to the Sacred Tree
ritual depictions. His body, beard, and other features are highly stylized.

This bas-relief of a courtier bearing arms (Figs. 15–16, pp. 31–32) has also been located in Room S (see Figs. 3, 13). Twenty-nine stone slabs originally decorated the walls of Room S. Rooms S and T probably functioned as a reception suite of sorts, and they share many similarities in their decoration and in the height of the Standard Inscription that runs across the figures in a band of nineteen lines.

In his left hand, the courtier holds a bow, and in the right, a mace. He wears a sword at his waist, its scabbard adorned with heads of lions, and a quiver of arrows hangs from his shoulder. He is beardless, denoting his status as a courtier, but he retains the highly stylized curled hair worn by the king and guardian spirits, which falls obliquely onto his shoulder. The figure also wears the large earring, wrist bracelet, and arm bracelet found on the *apkallu* in Figure 14. The garments cover most of the body, but his arms, hands, and feet all express the common conventions of Assyrian art. The courtier also has the small decorative incisions common in Room S and seen also on Yale's *apkallu*. These incisions are found on the front of his garment around the legs and on the quiver, and some show the Sacred Tree ritual (Fig. 16). Red and black paint is preserved on the sandals of this figure, as in the *apkallu* in Figure 13.

This figure is unique because it is part of the only representation of the king flanked by two courtiers on large bas-reliefs in this, the South Wing of the palace. Behind each courtier was a Sacred Tree; the one associated with this figure is partly preserved at Yale (Fig. 17, p. 33).

Figure 15

Facing page: Figure 16
This page: Figure 17

The relief shown in Figure 18 (p. 35) is on a smaller scale than the previous two examples discussed. It is from Room I of the palace (see Figs. 3, 13 lower), where the program of relief-decoration was different from that in Room S, where Yale's two larger bas-reliefs were located.

The figural decoration in Room I was arranged in two rows, one above the other, with a register of Standard Inscription between them, in a fairly uniform pattern. On the bottom row, eagle-headed figures like this one were depicted performing the Sacred Tree ritual. On the top row, kneeling *apkallu* (Figs. 19–20, pp. 37–39) performing a ritual in a symmetrical pattern, facing one another. Separating the registers was a band of Standard Inscription, two lines of which can be seen on the upper part of this fragment of a larger slab.

The eagle-headed *apkallu* is a common figure in Near Eastern art, with parallels in terra-cotta figures and on the decoration of cylinder seals. The basic function of eagle-headed figures is thought to be similar to that of the winged, human-headed *apkallu* already discussed.

This eagle-headed figure is facing right and carrying a pail in his lower hand and the ceremonial cone in his upper hand. He is performing the Sacred Tree ritual on the one half of the stylized tree that survives here. His crest reaches into the bottom of the Standard Inscription. The figure is wearing a short tunic with a belt and a long mantle with fringe decoration, as well as a necklace, bracelet, and armband.

No visible paint remains on the stone's surface, but traces of paint have been found on similar figures elsewhere in the palace, suggesting that it once had a vivid color scheme of red, blue, black, yellow, and white.

Facing page: Figure 18

Here we see a small, kneeling, human-headed *apkallu* and an almost complete Sacred Tree, which is said to belong on the *apkallu*'s left (Figs. 19–20, pp. 37–39). According to scholars, these two fragments were originally placed above the eagle-headed figure shown in Figure 18 in Room I of the Northwest Palace (see Figs. 3, 13 upper). Altogether the fragments would thus have formed one vertical panel in their original configuration, joined by the Standard Inscription that originally ran between them but was discarded when the slab was cut for shipment.

The human-headed, winged *apkallu*, like the eagle-headed *apkallu* in Figure 18, is smaller in scale than the ones in Figures 14 and 15 because it was part of the program of bas-relief in two registers in Room I. Unlike the eagle-headed *apkallu*, this figure is kneeling and is not employing the bucket and cone in the performance of the Sacred Tree ritual. Instead, his elongated hands seem to be outstretched in a worshipping or caring gesture.

The hands and feet follow traditional Assyrian methods of rendering human motion, although here the appendages seem less than naturalistic. The *apkallu* wears a necklace, earring, bracelets, and a short tunic under a one-shouldered fur cloak. He is barefoot. As with the *apkallu* in Figure 18, no visible paint remains on the figure, although it was once vibrantly decorated.

The importance of the sacred tree to Assyrian iconography and religion is a puzzling feature of the palace's artistic program and has given rise to various interpretations of its meaning, as discussed above. In the context of Room I, the tree plays prominently and is presented numerous times, both as an object of worship and as an essential figure holding the symmetry of the scene together.

Figure 19

Figure 20

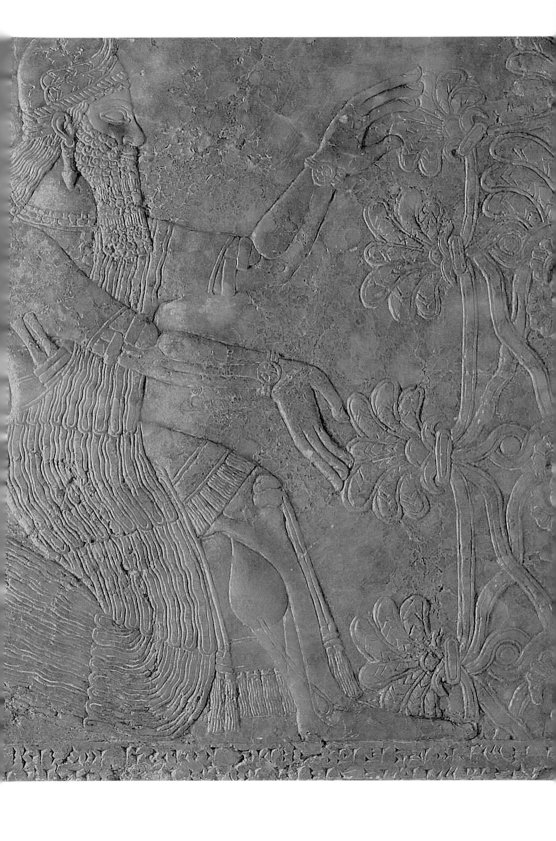

NOTES ON THE TEXT

p. 4   Quotation from Standard Inscription. Excerpted from translation by S. M. Paley, *King of the World* (Brooklyn, N.Y., 1976), 125–32.

p. 17–18   Dwight W. Marsh to Professor A. L. Perry, Williams College, November 29, 1882: Williams College Archives and Special Collections, Courtesy Williams College Museum of Art.

pp. 18–19   All quotes from Dwight W. Marsh to Rev. Mark Hopkins, President of Williams College. August 7, 1855: Williams College Archives and Special Collections, Courtesy Williams College Museum of Art.

p. 20   William Frederic Williams, 1851 (ca. July 20), as quoted in E. Dunbar, *Talcott Williams: Gentleman of the Fourth Estate* (Brooklyn, N.Y. 1936), 47.

p. 21   William Frederic Williams to Rev. Leonard Bacon, June 15, 1853: Yale University Art Gallery Archives.

pp. 22–23   Williams excerpts: Ibid.

p. 26   Edward Hitchcock, president of Amherst College, in a speech opening the "Nineveh Gallery" at Amherst, 1857: quoted in J. B. Stearns, *Reliefs from the Palace of Ashurnasirpal II* (Graz, 1961), 3.

NOTES ON THE ILLUSTRATIONS

Frontispiece: Relief of a Human-Headed *Apkallu*, Assyrian, Palace of Assurnasirpal II, 9th century B.C. Alabaster. Yale University Art Gallery, 1854.1 Photograph: Alex Contreras.

Opposite page 1: Relief of a Human-Headed Kneeling *Apkallu* (detail), Assyrian, Palace of Assurnasirpal II, 9th century B.C. Alabaster. Yale University Art Gallery, 1854.4-5. Photograph: Alex Contreras.

Fig. 1   Map of Assyria and surrounding region. Courtesy of Lesley Tucker and Ahree Lee.

Fig. 2   Statue of King Assurnasirpal II holding the symbols of sovereignty (detail). From the temple of Ishtar at Nimrud. Assyrian, 874–860 B.C.E. Limestone. London, British Museum. Photo: Werner Forman/Art Resource, NY.

Fig. 3   Plan of Northwest Palace of Ashur-nasir-pal II, Nimrud, after a plan by R. P. Sobolewski, reproduced with permission.

Fig. 4   Human-headed bull colossus from Nimrud, Northwest Palace, Room S, Door e, no. 2; 312 x 312 x 66 cm. Metropolitan Museum of Art 32.143.1. Photo: Metropolitan Museum of Art, Gift of John D. Rockefeller, Jr., 1932.

Fig. 5   Rendering of the Throne Room (Looking west into an adjacent anteroom) of the Northwest Palace of Ashur-nasir-pal II, Nimrud (ca. 9th century B.C.), extracted from the Learning Sites interactive 3D computer model of the Palace (based on archaeological data and interpretations provided by Samuel M. Paley, Donald H. Sanders, Alison B. Snyder, and Richard P. Sobolewski); copyright 2002 Learning Sites, Inc.

Fig. 6   Assurnasirpal II in royal progress, detail from Assurnasirpal II's siege of a city, Palace of Assurnasirpal II, London, British Museum. Photo: Erich Lessing/Art Resource, NY.

Fig. 7   Relief of a Human-Headed *Apkallu* (detail), Assyrian, Palace of Assurnasirpal II, 9th century B.C. Alabaster. Yale University Art Gallery, 1854.1. Photograph: Alex Contreras.

Fig. 8   "Reception of Nineveh Sculptures at the British Museum," *Illustrated London News* 28 (February 1852): 184.

Fig. 9   Austen Henry Layard's reconstruction of Ashurnasirpal's throne room, Northwest Palace, Room B, A. H. Layard, Monuments of Nineveh (London, 1849), pl. 2.

Fig. 10   William Frederic Williams, from E. Dunbar, *Talcott Williams: Gentleman of the Fourth Estate* (Brooklyn, N.Y., 1936).

Fig. 11   Relief of an Eagle-Headed *Apkallu* (detail), Assyrian, Palace of Assurnasirpal II, 9th century B.C. Alabaster. Yale University Art Gallery, 1854.3. Photograph: Alex Contreras.

Fig. 12   Relief of a Human-Headed *Apkallu* (detail), Assyrian, Palace of Assurnasirpal II, 9th century B.C. Alabaster. Yale University Art Gallery, 1854.1. Photograph: Alex Contreras.

Fig. 13   Reliefs from Rooms S & I, Northwest Palace of Assurnasirpal II, reconstruction (detail) from S. M. Paley and R. P. Sobolewski, *The Reconstruction of the Relief Representations and Their Positions in the Northwest-Palace at Kalhu (Nimrud) II* (Mainz, 1987), pl. 1 (Room I) and pl. 2 (Room S).

Fig. 14   Relief of a Human-Headed *Apkallu* (detail), Assyrian, Palace of Assurnasirpal II, 9th century B.C. Alabaster. Yale University Art Gallery, 1854.1. Photograph: Alex Contreras.

Fig. 15   Relief of a Courtier, Assyrian, Palace of Assurnasirpal II, 9th century B.C. Alabaster. Yale University Art Gallery, 1854.2.1. Photograph: Alex Contreras.

Fig. 16   Relief of a Courtier (detail), Assyrian, Palace of Assurnasirpal II, 9th century B.C. Alabaster. Yale University Art Gallery, 1854.2.1. Photograph: Alex Contreras.

Fig. 17   Relief of part of a Sacred Tree, Assyrian, Palace of Assurnasirpal II, 9th century B.C. Alabaster. Yale University Art Gallery 1854.2.2. Photograph: Alex Contreras.

Fig. 18   Relief of an Eagle-Headed *Apkallu*, Assyrian, Palace of Assurnasirpal II, 9th century B.C. Alabaster. Yale University Art Gallery, 1854.3. Photograph: Alex Contreras.

Fig. 19   Relief of a Human-Headed Kneeling *Apkallu* (detail), Assyrian, Palace of Assurnasirpal II, 9th century B.C. Alabaster. Yale University Art Gallery, 1854.4. Photograph: Alex Contreras.

Fig. 20   Relief of a Human-Headed Kneeling *Apkallu*, Assyrian, Palace of Assurnasirpal II, 9th century B.C. Alabaster. Yale University Art Gallery, 1854.4–1854.5. Photograph: Alex Contreras.

SELECTED READING

Mehmet-Ali Ataç, "Visual Formula and Meaning in Neo-Assyrian Relief Sculpture," *Art Bulletin* 88, no. 1 (2006): 67–101.

R. D. Barnett, *Assyrian Sculpture in the British Museum* (Toronto, 1975).

P. Bartl, "Des Königs neue Kleider? Die Orthostatsreliefs Assurnasirpal II und ihre Ritzversierungen," *Alter Orient* 6 (2005): 4–11.

P. Bartl, "Layard's Drawings of the Incised Decorations on the Nimrud Reliefs Compared with the Originals," *Iraq* 67 (2005): 4–11.

J. E. Curtis and J. E. Reade, *Art and Empire: Treasures from Assyria in the British Museum*, exhibition catalogue, Metropolitan Museum of Art (New York, 1995).

C. J. Gadd, *The Stones of Assyria* (London, 1936), 245, pl. 3.

A. K. Grayson, *Assyrian Rulers of the Early First Millenium* B.C. *I* (1114–859 B.C.) (Toronto, 1991).

J. Oates and D. Oates, *Nimrud: An Assyrian Imperial City Revealed* (London, 2001).

S. M. Paley, *King of the World* (Brooklyn, N.Y., 1976).

S. M. Paley and R. P. Sobolewski, *The Reconstruction of the Relief Representations and Their Positions in the Northwest Palace at Kalhu (Nimrud) II* (Mainz, 1987).

S. Parpola, "The Assyrian Tree of Life: Tracing the Origins of Jewish Monotheism and Greek Philosophy," *Journal of Near Eastern Studies* 52 (1993): 161–208.

B. N. Porter, "Sacred Trees, Date Palms, and the Royal Persona of Ashurnasirpal II," *Journal of Near Eastern Studies* 52 (1993): 129–39.

J. E. Reade, "Twelve Assurnasirpal Reliefs," *Iraq* 27 (1965): 119–34.

J. E. Reade, *Assyrian Sculpture* (Cambridge, Mass., 1983).

J. M. Russell, *From Nineveh to New York* (New Haven, Conn., 1997).

J. M. Russell, "The Program of the Palace of Assurnasirpal II at Nimrud: Issues in the Research and Presentation of Assyrian Art," *American Journal of Archaeology* 102 (1998): 655–715.

J. M. Russell, *The Writing on the Wall: Studies in the Architectural Context of Late Assyrian Palace Inscriptions* (Winona Lake, Ind., 1999).

J. B. Stearns, *Reliefs from the Palace of Assurnasirpal II* (Graz, 1961).

T. J. Wilkinson, E. B. Wilkinson, J. Ur, and M. Altaweel, "Landscape and Settlement in the Neo-Assyrian Empire," *Bulletin of the American Schools of Oriental Research* 340 (2005): 23–56.

On Reverend Williams, nineteenth-century university education, and the missionaries' acquisition campaign:

E. Dunbar, *Talcott Williams: Gentleman of the Fourth Estate* (Brooklyn, N.Y., 1936).

D. H. Finnie, *Pioneers East: The Early American Experience in the Middle East* (Cambridge, Mass., 1967).

J. B. Stearns, *Reliefs from the Palace of Assurnasirpal II* (Graz, 1961), 1–17.

L. Stevenson, *Scholarly Means to Evangelical Ends: The New Haven Scholars and the Transformation of Higher Learning in America, 1830–1890* (Baltimore, 1986).